Knowing there is no hope to
succeed with a dreary sombre recipe,
design had been underway for some time at ➪

They were aiming to create
an art recipe which really works...
and which really works to inspire success,
where the challenge is the fun for

ONE AND ALL

POULTRY LOT DESIGN STUDIO

4CHIKN

Patricia the Architect, a head designer of
Poultry Lot Design Studio is not here just now.
For she has just departed, not by her car 4CHIKN,
but by her trusty bike to make a special delivery to the Mer's ...

ONE AND ALL   #001 Croissant Create

Poultry Lot Design Studio proudly present the Golden Plan for

ONE AND ALL

to savour the success of home made croissants.

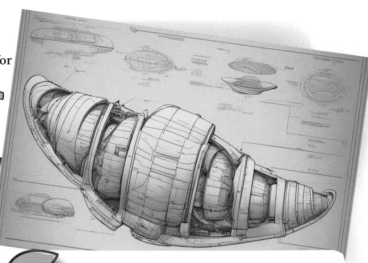

CONTENTS

PATRICIA

THE ARCHITECT

Tired of observing second rate design, Patricia as a young chook drew the line to accept nothing less than exemplary. First rate excellence is her creed. So much so that a first rate batch of croissants we shall christen as a 'Patricia Batch'...

SERVES
All Things Good

TIME
Patience

METHOD
Precision & Care

DISASTER
Word Unknown

TEAM
11/10

Immersive
Timpani

A sport where you really get into it! Immersive Timpani is a sport which Patricia is a world champion in.

Some liken her style to whirling surf, while others describe it more as a washing machine hurricane.

Right now sounds like here comes a big whirling suspenseful timpani roll...

For most recipes at this stage
build up making Croissants
into a colossal epic struggle...
feared by even professional pastry chefs.

They make you dread the
very idea of beginning.

To even attempt such a feat
would not only require the
colossal strength of a gladiator,
but every superpower of a superhero!

■ BUTTERMAN   super hero

■ CROISSANT-ACUS   gladiator

But this recipe will show you that
to make Croissants we need be neither
Croissant-acus, nor Butterman.

For this Golden Plan
requires no superpowers!

BUT Croissant production is precise.
⇐ It requires Patrician precision.

DO study the methods and
follow the steps carefully.

DO NOT rush, cut corners
or be short of time!

♩ ONE AND ALL   #001 Croissant Create

SOBRIQUET

Every design project requires a SOBRIQUET (soh-bri-kay).

This is a French word for a nickname.

But more than just a nickname, it is one which plays upon and gives insight by describing a persons character - or in this case, by describing a Design Project.

This is design sobriquet - PARIS 212.

PARIS 212 - how perfectly apt for Croissants!
But being a sobriquet,
the P.A.R.I.S. is not actually the City...

Pastry **A**rt **R**ecipe **I**nspiring **S**uccess

And why the 212?

12 steps **2** make **12** Croissants

PARIS 212 started the day The Mer's came in to discuss achieving their custom dream design with Patricia.

For they shared a simple desire for an easily workable Croissant recipe which was not colourless and forlorn...

And thats how they got their Sobriquet -
The Custom-Mers!

The Mer's were the customers for Patricia and this custom design project, but the Mer's themselves knew all about customers and custom projects.

For their business was in the custom handling of Puffball Dreams ... those dreams created when you close your eyes and make a wish as you blow the Puffball seeds of a Dandelion away...

THE MERS

The Mer's had observed that traditionally the seeds of a Puffball could journey for up to 24 hours and 5 miles. The Mer's also noted how this created a delay between when the custom dream was made, and when the custom dream was delivered to the customer.

So the Mer's invented a portable scanner to custom read each dream the instant of puff! This enabled the dream to be packed and shipped 24 hours before their competitors were even near starting- which made their business very successful to their customers!

The very careful observation of the instant a wish floats away...

Great design begins with perfect ingredients...

1st perfect ingredient...   a great designer like Patricia

2nd perfect ingredient...   great client's like the Mer's

3rd perfect ingredients...   find these ingredients and lets begin...

INGREDIENTS

01	PLAIN FLOUR...	4 cups,
		2 tablespoons
02	SUGAR...	1/4 cup
03	SALT...	2 Teaspoons
04	DRY YEAST...	1 Tablespoon
05	EGG...	1 of
06	BUTTER...	60g (1/4 cup),
		350g (1+1/2 cups)
07	MILK...	1+ 1/2 cups,
		30ml

STEP 01

Measure out into a mixing bowl -

- 4 cups of Plain Four
- 1/4 cup of Sugar
- 2 Teaspoons of Salt
- 1 Tablespoon of Dry Yeast

Give a good stir to combine well, then add

- 60g (1/4 cup) Butter Cubes

Rub butter into the dry ingredients, then add

- 1 and a 1/2 cups of milk

Add little amounts of milk as you stir,

before 2 minutes of good hard stirring.

It should now be combined into a ball.

Before Step 2,
make sure you read
KNEADING on Page 09
very very carefully

STEP 02

After reading Kneading, put the pastry on brown paper lightly sprinkled with flour. Knead good and hard for at least 5 minutes. Each time you complete Step A to D give the pastry a 1/4 turn and repeat, repeat, repeat.

Keep going until it passes the Poke Test

Always keep the dough,
your hands, the rolling pin and
the work surface lightly floured -
but not too much flour to
dry out the dough.

POKE TEST

Simply give the pastry ball ...
a little poke with your finger...
if it bounces back... it is ready!
If not, repeat Steps A to E
until it does bounce back

ONE AND ALL   #001 Croissant Create

If the pastry becomes too sticky when kneading sprinkle a little flour on it- but don't use too much as we don't want dry dough

A

B

C

D

E

KNEADING

STEP A	With the palm of your hand push firmly down into the ball
STEP B	Keeping your palm down push away from yourself and stretch
STEP C	Stretch as far as you can and then curl fingers down
STEP D	Lift up the end of the dough and fold it back onto itself
STEP E	Give the dough a quarter turn and repeat again from Step A

Work to get a nice rolling rhythm going... Really immerse yourself in the rhythm of the Kneading!

ONE AND ALL   #001 Croissant Create

30 MINUTE REST

Place the pastry back in the bowl and loosely cover with aluminium foil. Now we place the pastry into the fridge for 30 minutes to rest... and we can too.

If an air bubble appears in your dough at anytime when rolling it out - pop it with a toothpick and lightly rub a little flour where it popped

STEP 03

Now we roll out the pastry to a 36 x 25cm (14x10 inch) rectangle with equal thickness. And now unless you just happen to have a steam roller tractor, we'll use a rolling pin!

The pastry wants to roll into a round shape, but simply squish the corners back square. When roughly the right size, use the pizza cutter to get straight sharp edges all round.

24 HOUR REST

Place the pastry onto a baking tray and loosely cover it with aluminium foil. Now we place the pastry into the fridge for our first big rest of 24 hours!

ONE AND ALL   *#001 Croissant Create*

STEP 04

Measure out and place in a mixing bowl -

- 350g (1 1/2 cups) Butter Cubes
- 2 Tablespoons of Plain Flour

Rub the butter into the flour to thoroughly combine and make one big butter ball.

Roll out the butter to 18 x 25cm (7x10 inch). When roughly the right size, use the pizza cutter to get straight sharp edges all round. This is our Butter Tourrage.

30 MINUTE REST

Place the Tourrage uncovered onto a baking tray and place into the fridge for 30 minutes.

Just perfect time to read Inspector Louis on Page 13, the finest Investigator there ever will be...

INSPECTOR LOUIS

Bonjour, I am Inspector Louis, Private Investigator Extraordinaire! Todays case is without doubt some of my most important work to date as I investigate two important terms for Croissant baking. My client is Patricia the Chicken, and I know her standards are high and she will want things done right.

La Official Unofficial Investigation Service **L.O.U.I.S.** Private Investigator Paris

MAJOR INVESTIGATION
DÉTREMPE AND TOURRAGE

The names of DÉTREMPE and TOURRAGE had come across my desk. I had no knowledge of these names.

Were these the names of two master criminals about to land a major heist? I set off with haste to investigate.

I had asked around on the street for any intel or leads, but I was getting nowhere... when a wise chicken told me DÉTREMPE was going to encase/ wrap up TOURRAGE!

Wrapping up - bringing to an end? Alarmed I rushed only to discover -

DÉTREMPE - is the pastry dough
TOURRAGE - is the butter block

And so I had discovered that in **C**roissant production, the **T**ourrage (butter block) is **E**ncased/ wrapped up by the **D**étrempe (pastry).

ACTED - Looking down my notes it was there in plain sight... just like in a movie... which got me thinking about... Movies...

DÉTREMPE + TOURRAGE...
What an idea for a movie of perfect combination just like **ROMEO + JULIET**... star crossed butter + pastry ... though hopefully a little less tragedy for our batch of croissants!

CONCLUSION to report back to Patricia
I am going to see a movie tonight. What better way to spend the time during a 24 hour rest.

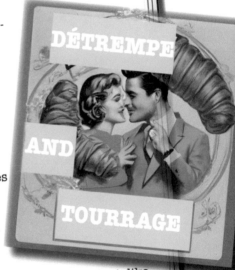

DÉTREMPE AND TOURRAGE

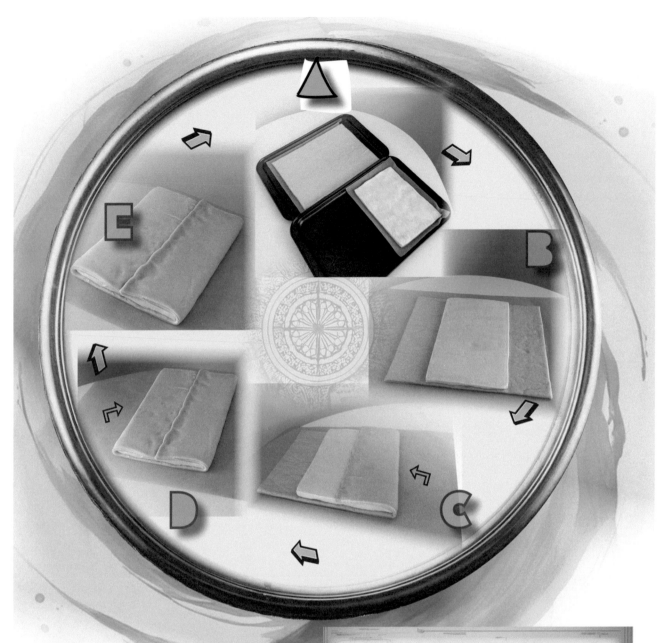

Note how our
TOURRAGE (18 x 25cm)
is exactly half the size of our
DÉTREMPE (36 x 25cm).

STEP 05

STEP A	Take out our DÉTREMPE and TOURRAGE rectangles
STEP B	Place the butter rectangle in the middle of the pastry
STEP C	Fold the pastry over from the right side to the centre
STEP D	Fold the pastry over from the left side to the centre
STEP E	Then press the pastry together in the middle to join

STEP 06

Now we roll out our Croissant pastry
to a 50 x 25cm (20x10 inch) rectangle.
Start by rolling from the shorter side which
rolls from 18cm (7 inch) to 25cm (10 inch).
Keep rolling until our rulers say a precise
50 x 25cm(20x10 inch) rectangle.

Before Step 7,
make sure you read
LAMINATE on Page 16
very very carefully

STEP 7.1

Now, as per Laminate on Page 16, we fold
the right side, and then the left side over,
and now we have laminated for the first time!
And who thought we would be cooking with
old school rulers ! But it is vital equipment for
precise dimensions - just don't press too hard.

Recognise
Rulers

Presented in worthy recognition
from the great Rulers of history to
our trusty wooden rulers at school.

And in tribute to 30cm rulers ...
for they don't make them any longer...
Cluck, cluck, cluck... get it?

ONE AND ALL   #001 Croissant Create

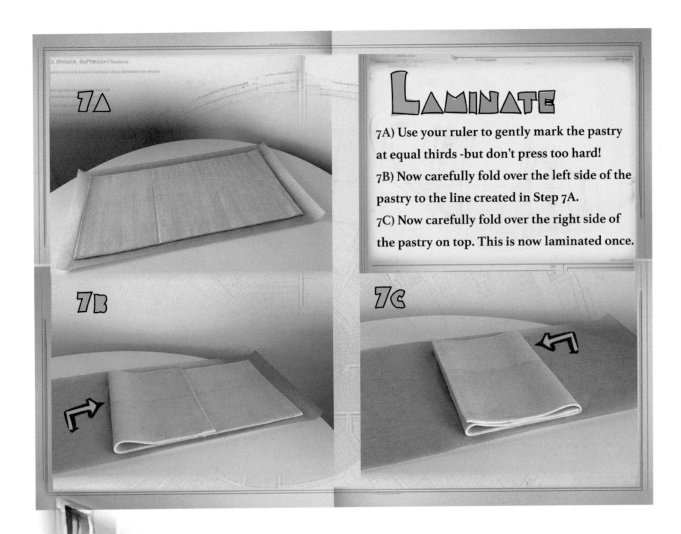

LAMINATE

7A) Use your ruler to gently mark the pastry at equal thirds -but don't press too hard!

7B) Now carefully fold over the left side of the pastry to the line created in Step 7A.

7C) Now carefully fold over the right side of the pastry on top. This is now laminated once.

STEP 7.2

Repeat Step 06 by rolling out our pastry back to a 50 x 25cm (20x10 inch) rectangle. Then, as per Laminate (above) again fold the left side, and then the right side over. We have now laminated for the 2nd time!

The dough should be cold at any step of this creation when working with it. If it seems to have lost it's cool, place it in the fridge until it is cool again

MER$

30 MINUTE REST

Place the pastry onto a baking tray and loosely cover it with aluminium foil.

Now we place the pastry into the fridge for 30 minutes and yes again... Rest time!

STEP 7.3

Now once more we repeat Step 06 by rolling our Croissant pastry back out to a 50 x 25cm (20x10 inch) rectangle.

Then as per Laminate (page 16) we fold the left side over and then the right side over. Now we've laminated for the 3rd + final time!

24 HOUR REST

Place the pastry onto a baking tray and loosely cover it with aluminium foil.

Now we place the pastry into the fridge for our second big rest of 24 hours!

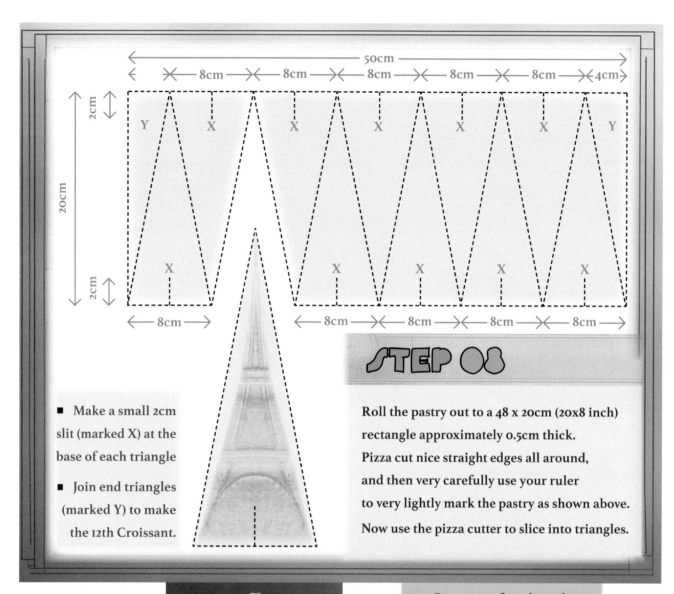

50cm
8cm | 8cm | 8cm | 8cm | 8cm | 4cm

2cm

20cm

Y X X X X X Y

X X X X X

2cm

8cm | 8cm | 8cm | 8cm | 8cm

- Make a small 2cm slit (marked X) at the base of each triangle

- Join end triangles (marked Y) to make the 12th Croissant.

STEP 08

Roll the pastry out to a 48 x 20cm (20x8 inch) rectangle approximately 0.5cm thick.

Pizza cut nice straight edges all around, and then very carefully use your ruler to very lightly mark the pastry as shown above.

Now use the pizza cutter to slice into triangles.

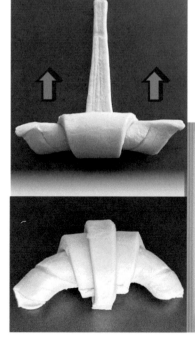

Be super soft and gentle with the pastry so we don't flatten the layers we've spent so long creating

STEP 09

Separate the triangles and roll them up! Start by rolling at the wide end, and make sure that the tip finishes underneath so they don't unravel during cooking.

Place Croissants onto final baking tray/s allowing room for them to expand.

ONE AND ALL   #001 Croissant Create

STEP 10

Now loosely cover the Croissant baking tray with aluminium foil, and then place out on the benchtop to PROOF for 1 to 3 hours. This time required depends on the seasonal temperature - shorter time required in hot temperatues/ longer for cool temperatures.

30 MINUTE REST

The PROOF is complete once the Croissants have roughly doubled in size.

Then they're ready to be placed into the fridge for the final rest!

STEP 11

Turn your oven on to 375°F / 190°C.

Meanwhile measure and and place in a bowl -
- 1 egg
- 2 Tablespoons of Milk

Mix thoroughly with a fork and then pastry brush this egg wash onto each Croissant.

STEP 12

Place the tray into the pre-warmed oven. Bake for 9 minutes, and then turn the tray around to bake for a final 9 minutes. When the Croissants are golden brown, remove from the oven and leave them to cool for 2 minutes...

Now it is time for One and All to saviour and enjoy our homemade Croissants...

Sure looks like a true 'Patricia Batch' to me!

And time now for Patricia to see if her Custom-Mers are happy with the results! Lets see....

PODIUM

PANDEMONIUM

If Croissant making was a sporting event, these two look like they have well and truly just won a gold medal!

SERVES	TIME		TOTAL TIME
12 Croissants	A few days ...		All worth it now!
		DISASTER None - a recipe in success!	
	METHOD - Great design!		

PODIUM — the celebration

After all that kneading, rolling and resting this is what we've been striving for... Pandemonium! Tasting like we've all just won gold, it's that one moment of first bite flakey croissant for

- Best eaten within an hour or 2 of baking!
- Not a gold medal but a golden Croissant!
- decisions... Raspberry Jam or plain?
- Enjoy... for you have earned it!

ONE AND ALL ...

ONE AND ALL   *#001 Croissant Create*

The Mer's prove what better way to create a dream,
than by using dreams to benefit one and all.
For through their good fortune pioneering the
instant logistical handling of custom dreams,
they created this great design project.
And for Patricia proved to truly be great ...

CUSTOM-MERS

The Croissants created taste best eaten on
the same day as baking but can stay for in the fridge for
up to a week- keep in the freezer if storing longer.

If you want to get a batch ready for a certain time,
as you have probably worked out already,
you to have plan your time ahead.

Time now to put my
chicken feet up and have
a relaxing dream of my own...

Poultry Lot Design will be back soon,
but for now it's the end of

ONE AND ALL

#001 Croissant Create

It's probably just a dream,

and I might miss the poultry lot,

but I guess such Croissant success...

Leads me from the chicken shed,

to my own frilly chateau life...

but it won't change me much...

CROISSANT NOTES

CROISSANT NOTES

CROISSANT NOTES

Made in United States
Troutdale, OR
12/09/2024

26219598R00017